How to Be a

Medieval Knight

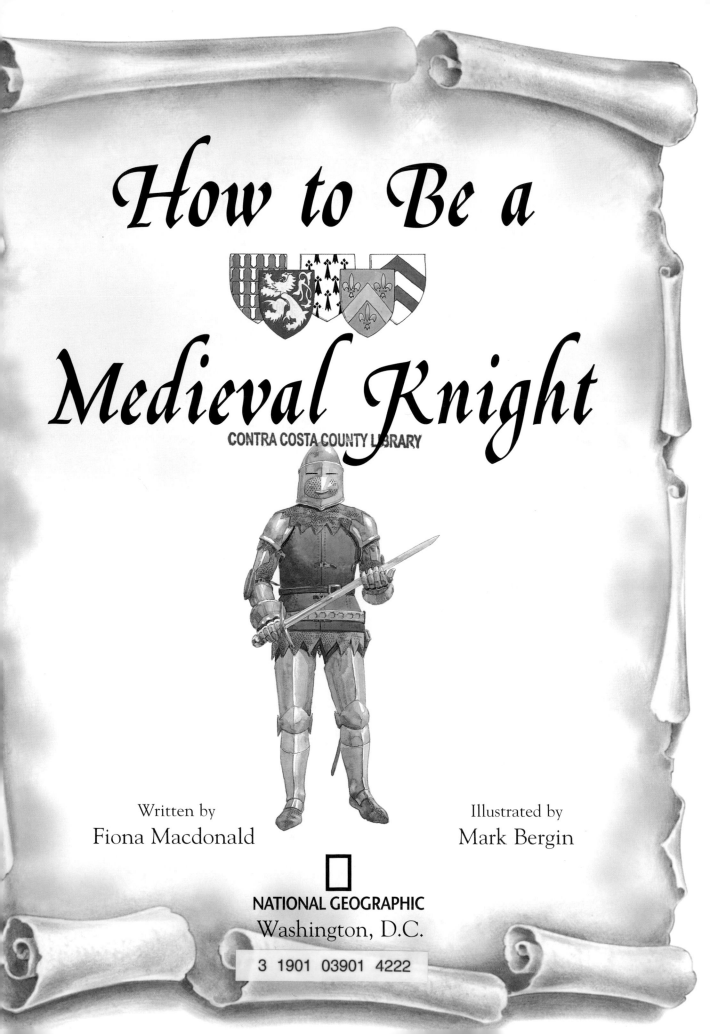

Written by
Fiona Macdonald

Illustrated by
Mark Bergin

NATIONAL GEOGRAPHIC
Washington, D.C.

© The Salariya Book Company Ltd MMIV
Please visit the Salariya Book Company at:
www.salariya.com

First published in North America in 2005 by
NATIONAL GEOGRAPHIC SOCIETY
1145 17th Street, N.W.
Washington, D.C. 20036-4688

Trade ISBN: 0-7922-3619-X
Library ISBN: 0-7922-3634-3

Library of Congress Cataloging-in-Publication Data available on request.

Printed in China

Series created and designed by David Salariya
Penny Clarke, Consultant Editor
Karen Barker Smith, Editor

For the National Geographic Society
Bea Jackson, Art Director
Virginia Ann Koeth, Project Editor

Chris Gravett, Fact Consultant
Former Curator at the British Museum and at the Royal Armouries in the Tower of London

Photographic credits

The Art Archive / Bibliothèque Municipale Rouen / Dagli
Orti: 23
The Art Archive / Bodleian Library Oxford / The Bodleian
Library: 19
The Art Archive / British Library / British Library: 6, 8
The Art Archive / College of Arms / John Webb: 21

The Art Archive / Musée Condé Chantilly / Dagli Orti: 29

Every effort has been made to trace copyright holders.
The Salariya Book Company apologizes for any unintentional
omissions and would be pleased, in such cases, to add an
acknowledgment in future editions.

One of the world's largest nonprofit scientific and educational organizations, the National Geographic Society was founded in 1888
"for the increase and diffusion of geographic knowledge." Fulfilling this mission, the Society educates and inspires millions every day
through its magazines, books, television programs, videos, maps and atlases, research grants, the National Geographic Bee, teacher
workshops, and innovative classroom materials. The Society is supported through membership dues, charitable gifts, and income from
the sale of its educational products. This support is vital to National Geographic's mission to increase global understanding and pro-
mote conservation of our planet through exploration, research, and education.

For more information, please call 1-800-NGS LINE (647-5463) or write to the following address:
National Geographic Society
1145 17th Street N.W.
Washington, D.C. 20036-4688 U.S.A.
Visit the Society's Web site at www.nationalgeographic.com.

Knights Needed

Can you defend your king and country? This is your chance to become a member of a top fighting force.

There are vacancies for bold, brave knights to fight in European wars. Applicants must be young, male, physically fit, and strong. It helps to come from a noble or wealthy family, so you can afford your own warhorse, weapons, and armor. Riding and fighting skills preferred.

The job requirements are

- obeying orders from the king, royal princes, and great nobles on campaigns at home and abroad;

- excellent sword-fighting and horse-riding skills and knowledge of medieval armor and weapons;

- keeping law and order in peacetime;

- maintaining the proper image of a knight through chivalry, loyalty, and honor.

Apply in writing to the lord's castle.

Contents

What Applicants Should Know

For this job you will have to travel back to medieval Europe, around A.D. 1000–1500. That was when knights had castles, took part in tournaments, and fought in wars. In Europe, the ruling kings and princes were trying to capture each other's kingdoms. Most of their land was farmed by peasants, who grew wheat and barley and raised livestock. Goods were made by craftworkers at home and sold in local market towns. The Christian church was very powerful. Priests, monks, and nuns had the best education.

Medieval Europe

A.D. 1000–1500

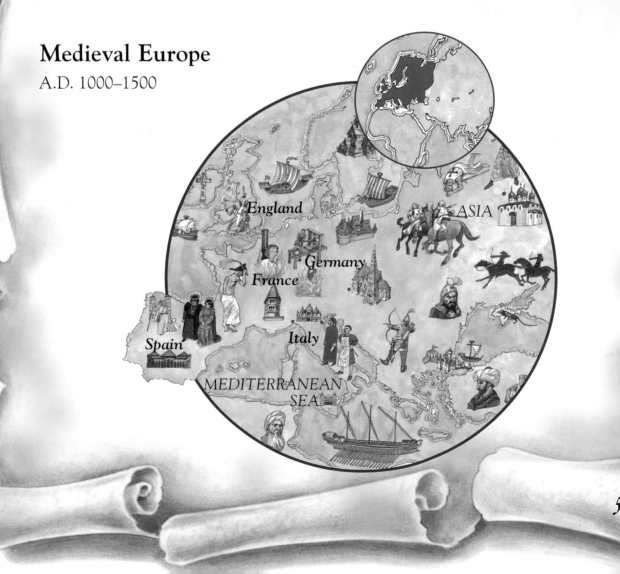

England

ASIA

Germany

France

Spain

Italy

MEDITERRANEAN
SEA

Ready to Fight?

Knights are expert fighting men. Do not apply to be one unless you can handle a life of hardship and danger. You may even face an early death. But being a knight can bring rich rewards, such as castles, treasures, and land. It is hard to beat the excitement of charging straight into battle alongside your comrades. And what other career can offer you fame, honor, and glory that lasts for hundreds of years?

Ready, willing, and able

▼ As a knight, you must always be ready to fight to defend your home, your family, your kingdom, and your honor. You also need a staff of grooms and squires to keep your horses, armor, and weapons ready for use at any time.

A knight wears his coat-of-arms on his shield

Role models

▶ Try to behave like the legendary King Arthur and the knights of the Round Table. Stories about their courage and chivalry are told by poets and minstrels.

Minstrels making music and singing songs at a banquet

A knight's honor

▶ Traditionally, knights value loyalty as much as fighting skills. Are you prepared to swear an oath to serve your king (*right*), even if it means losing your life?

A king and his loyal knights

I will fight you to the death!

Mercenaries

▼ You may meet a new kind of knight called a mercenary. He will fight for whoever will pay him and will even change sides if he is offered a richer reward. He brings his own army with him. The traditional knights do not approve of these mercenaries.

A mercenary and his army of soldiers for hire

A wealthy knight enjoying a banquet

A knight traveling with his grooms and squires

What's in a name?

▲ As a knight, you will have to get used to being called "sir." Being a knight is a sign of high status. Some wealthy and respected men are made knights even though they have never fought.

Are You from the Right Class?

Fighting is a man's job, so medieval women cannot become knights. As a boy, you are expected to be strong and brave. You are praised for being bold and daring—and scolded for showing any signs of cowardliness or weakness. You have a better chance of becoming a knight if your father is wealthy or a knight himself. Knights are usually from the top ranks of society, although a few are promoted just for their good fighting skills.

Rich and poor

▼ Medieval society is made up of a few rich, powerful people and many poorer ones. Eighty percent of the population is farmworkers, craftsmen, or servants.

Girl or boy?

▶ Parents are very pleased when boys are born. Male babies are always welcome, because they can inherit the family land and pass on the family name.

What shall I sing?

Peasants shown scything crops in a field on a medieval manuscript

Son and heir

▼ As a boy from a knight's family, you must do your duty from an early age. Sometimes this means spending long hours with adults, instead of playing with your friends. Listen carefully to all that goes on—it's never too soon to start learning.

Something about brave knights and battles!

Joan of Arc

Joan of Arc being burned at the stake

▲ Occasionally a few women break society's rules and ride off to war. One of the most famous of these women warriors was Joan of Arc. She lived in France from 1412–31. She believed God sent her messages telling her to lead the French army against the English soldiers who were occupying France. Joan won great victories, but she was betrayed and captured. The English said she she was listening to demons and breaking God's rules, and burned her to death.

A knight kneeling before his king at the royal court

The Crusades

◄ These are the epic religious wars fought by some Christian knights against Muslims in the Middle East and Spain. Will you be a Crusader, too?

For king and country

▲ Your training will teach you how to behave in the king's service and in the royal court. You must be fiercely loyal to your king. He needs knights to defend his kingdom. He may also call on you to go abroad, to conquer new lands.

Training to Be a Knight

Boys practicing with wooden models

Before you qualify as a knight, you will need many years of training. This starts at about eight years old and will continue until you are at least 21. First, you must work in another knight's household as a page (helper) or a groom (stable boy). You learn good manners, as well as useful information about warhorses. You might also learn to read and write. If you do well, you'll be promoted to squire. This is a responsible job. You act as a knight's trusted assistant and even go with him to war.

That's difficult in a suit of armor.

Becoming a knight takes a great deal of physical strength and athleticism

Leaving home

▶ Could you leave your home and family as a young boy to begin training as a knight?

A young boy sets off to seek his fortune as a knight

Practice makes perfect

▶ Practice your horsemanship and fighting skills at the quintain—a swinging weight on a tall pole.

Childhood training

◀ Develop your fighting spirit by playing war-games with other boys. These toy knights (*left*), made of wood, will teach you the importance of fast footwork and strong defense.

Watch out! This is only practice—not a real fight.

A squire helps a knight with his armor

◀ Between the ages of about 14 and 21 you will work as a squire, looking after a knight's equipment. Before battle, you help him put on his armor.

Special ceremonies

▲ Some extra-brave warriors are made knights on the battlefield, but most young men have to go through three special ceremonies before becoming a knight. First the warrior takes a bath that symbolizes the purification of his soul.

▲ Next, he spends a night praying at church, asking God to bless his future as a knight.

▼ Finally he is tapped on the shoulder with a sword by the king or a senior noble. This is called "accolade."

The Right Equipment

Becoming a knight is usually very expensive. As well as a warhorse, weapons, and armor, you need a tent and baggage horses for use on campaign. For peacetime feasts, and for attending the royal court, you will need fine clothes made of quality materials. You will also need to provide some weapons, clothes, and horses for the ordinary soldiers who go off to war with you.

Rich knight, poor knight

▼ If you're from a wealthy family, getting all the equipment you need should be easy. But if your family is poor, then you will have to capture these things in battle or win them as rewards.

> That's a fine suit of armor, sire.

Dressing for battle

▼ To get dressed in plate armor, you'll need help from your squire or groom. First of all, (a) put on woollen stockings, linen underpants, and a shirt. Over these, (b) wear your arming doublet and mail skirt. Then (c) put on the plate-armor, being careful to fasten all its buckled straps. Finally, add your helmet and gauntlets.

(a)

(b)

A knight's armor

▶ Your armor protects you from top to toe. A helmet covers your head and chain mail protects your arms and shoulders. Your chest, back, and elbows are shielded by metal plates as are your legs and feet. You wear a skirt of mail and metal gauntlets. All this armor can weigh over 45 pounds (20 kg).

And I'll wager that this is the finest sword in the kingdom, too!

(c)

Visor covers face

Shoulder guards

Mail collar

Breastplate under cloth covering

Gauntlets (gloves)

Couters (elbow guards)

Mail skirt

Cuisses (thigh guards)

Poleyns (knee guards)

Greaves (Lower leg guards)

Sabatons (foot guards)

Changing fashions

▲ Around A.D. 1000, knights wore suits of mail (*above left*). Around 1400, knights wear armor plate (*above right*). You need a good set of weapons: a mace, a lance, a long sword, and a dagger.

13

Surviving in Wartime

Expect to spend many months away from home when you are fighting a war. The battles often last less than a day, but it can take weeks before rival armies meet face to face. Troops travel very slowly—most soldiers go all the way on foot. Even if they have horses, they can't cover more than 25 miles (40 km) a day. Soldiers have to find food by raiding enemy land or by demanding "gifts" from their own countrymen. Ordinary people hide in terror whenever an army marches by.

Are you tough enough?

Spring and summer are the main fighting seasons, because muddy ground in winter makes travel difficult. Life in an army camp can be tough. Could you cope with damp, smelly tents, disgusting food, dirty water, fevers, and pests like lice and rats?

On to the next village, men!

Soldiers raid enemy towns as they march on toward the next battle

War at sea

▼ You may travel to war by ship or even fight on board. When that happens, soldiers will jump from ship to ship and attack one another on deck.

On the road to battle

▶ On campaign, you need to take all your weapons, armor, and supplies with you. Carry them on strong, sturdy packhorses or mules.

Roads and bridges

▶ When marching through enemy territory, you'll have to fight your way across well-defended bridges .

Looting

◀ Looting is cruel, but most armies do it. You'll have to control your men. They will know that larger towns (*below*) have rich treasures to steal: gold and silver crosses from churches, fine wools, silks and furs from craftsmen's shops, and hoards of jewels and gold coins from merchants.

▼ Soldiers in enemy territory will also attack the farmhouses of defenseless peasants (*below*). As well as seizing any stored food, they'll also drive away cows and sheep in order to kill and eat them in camp.

Stop! You've taken all we have!

Peasant houses contain plenty of food and livestock for soldiers to loot

Going into Battle

Battlefields can be very exciting. There's a real sense of anticipation as both sides pitch tents, make battle plans, and check their weapons. Before the battle begins, your leader will make a rousing speech, giving you great confidence in your own strength and skill. But the fighting itself is horrible. Even if you are not injured, many of your comrades will be wounded or killed.

Arrows, lances and crossbows

Longbows shoot a deadly rain of ▶ arrows on enemy troops. They terrify men and horses with their whistling sound. Knights charge into battle wielding long, heavy lances (*below*). They crash into ranks of enemy knights, hoping to knock them off their horses.

We will fight and win for our king and country!

Sword skills

▼ If you get thrown from your horse in battle, you'll have to fight on foot to save your life. Be prepared! You need expert training in swordsmanship to improve your chances of survival.

Helmets

▼ Knights can wear different styles of helmet in battle: (a) is a Norman helmet of about 1100; (b) is a German helmet from about 1350; (c) is a Swiss helmet from about 1350; (d) is another German helmet made around 1370.

(a)   (b)   (c)   (d)

▼ Crossbows are a new invention. They shoot short metal bolts that can smash through armor. On powerful crossbows, the string is winched taut with a windlass.

Foot soldiers use longbows to shoot arrows at the enemy from a distance

Bolts

Windlass

Mechanical crossbow

Foot soldiers

▶ You'll command troops of tough, brutal foot soldiers. They fight with bows and arrows. Foot soldiers stab and slash at their enemies with long pikes or halberds—sharp blades on poles.

A foot soldier fighting hard on the battlefield

Could You Stand a Siege?

Early castles were made of wood, but now, around 1400, most are built of stone. This means that siege warfare is growing more important. During a siege, armies surround an enemy castle or large city and try to smash their way in, using siege machines. If this fails, they simply wait for the enemy's food and water supplies to run out. Then the inhabitants are forced to surrender or starve to death.

Under siege

▼ Trapped in a castle siege, you seem to face certain death. But you fight the enemy, and you send messages by spies or carrier pigeons asking your allies to attack the enemy from behind.

Tunnels of fire

▶ Sappers (miners) dig tunnels close to castle walls, then light fires in them. This causes the collapse of the tunnel and the wall above it (*below*).

Sappers digging a tunnel

Plague

▶ Besiegers hurl dead rats at their enemies, hoping to spread the deadly plague. Humans are infected from being bitten by germ-carrying rat fleas.

Rats spread the plague

A *ballista shown on a 15th-century manuscript*

War machines

◀ The ballista shoots enormous arrows. It is operated by pulling back a huge wooden lever and then releasing it.

Mangonel

▲ Mangonels are large catapults used to hurl heavy stones through the air into castle walls. They are operated by expert army engineers.

Trebuchet

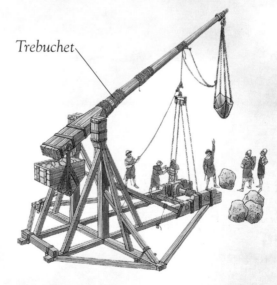

Keep attacking – the castle will soon be ours!

▼ Metal cannons have been used since around A.D. 1300. They fire deadly cannonballs but are very dangerous to use. Sometimes they explode, killing the soldiers nearby.

Cannon

▲ Trebuchets are more powerful and accurate than catapults, but less mobile. Trebuchets can fling heavy stones (up to 110 pounds [50 kg]) high over the top of castle walls.

Can You Win the Tournament?

Tournaments are grand mock battles and a favorite form of entertainment for knights and nobles. You get the chance to win fame, glory, and prizes. You have to "unhorse" your opponents without leaving your own saddle, but can also score points by striking them well or breaking your own lance against them. At first, tournaments were a way of training for war; they can still be very dangerous. Armed knights on armored horses charge headlong toward each other in the "lists"—a special arena.

Dress for the day

▼ Many important members of the noble classes attend tournaments. When invited to take part, you must look your best. Knights wear surcoats over their armor and horses wear coverings called "*caparisons*", which are decorated with the knight's coat-of-arms.

Heraldic crests

Your shield should be decorated ▶ with your coat-of-arms. These help to identify knights in battle and are badges of rank.

Aargh!

Knights jousting in a tournament

Heraldic shield and helmet crests from a medieval manuscript

Tents

▼ Knights and important nobles pitch their tents around the field at the tournament. Try to find time to visit each one and politely pay your respects. It's a good way of getting to know powerful people who may be able to help your career.

It's my turn now— wish me luck.

Risky sports

◄ As the Middle Ages progressed, tournaments become less dangerous. Swords and lances are blunted by the mid-12th century and by the 15th century a central barrier stops the horses from crashing into one another. Still, bruises and broken bones are common injuries.

A lady's love

► Your sweetheart may give you her scarf or her glove. Keep it as a token of her love for you. Wear it in your helmet with pride.

Rich Rewards

Getting rich is not the main reason for being a knight, but there are rewards if you are lucky in war. If you capture important prisoners on the battlefield, their families will pay you money to set them free. Fight bravely for your king and he might reward you with houses, castles, or land. You could also get lots of treasures by raiding enemy houses and churches—but this is against the knight's code of honor.

A knight's castle

▼ A castle is a knight's greatest reward. You can capture one or build your own if you make enough money. It will stand as a monument to your strength and fighting skills.

The lord's rooms

▼ If you get to be lord of the castle, you live in your own rooms with a team of servants to look after you.

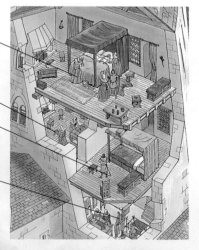

Master bedroom

Wardrobe room

Bedroom

Spinning and weaving rooms

Masons are skilled workers. ▶ They have a number of tools to help them work in both wood and stone. In the picture opposite, from the 15th century, a mason carries some of the tools of his trade.

Building a castle

► Master masons sketch the castle plans on drawing floors made of plaster. The masons give instructions to the building workers.

A mason tells castle builders what to do

Workers digging castle foundations

◄ A castle with solid foundations will stand strong for many years to come.

► Workers cut blocks of building stone into shape (*right*), and mix lime and sand to make mortar (*below*).

Workers prepare stone and mortar

▼ Carpenters make wooden frames to support arches while they are being built.

Hammer

Shovel

Ax

Life in Peacetime

A knight does not spend all his life fighting. During peacetime you go to meetings of parliament or to advise the king at the royal court. You give feasts for neighbors and important people in your community. You serve as a judge and also help keep law and order. You spend a great deal of your time giving orders to the people who run the farms on your estate. Also, some knights were successful merchants.

Running your estate

▲ Peasants on your estate live in small cottages with gardens. They grow vegetables and keep animals. In return, they work on your fields or pay you rent. All taxes must be paid on time. Your servants should keep proper records of this.

Home comforts

▼ When you return home after a long and busy day, your servants welcome you. They wash your feet and offer you food and drink.

Servants waiting on a weary knight

A fair mind

▼ A knight must oversee meetings of the village court. You settle arguments between neighbors and set punishment for minor crimes.

A kind heart

▼ Poor people will stand outside your castle gate, asking for food or money. As an honorable knight, it is your duty to help them.

A knight helping the poor

Entertaining

▼ When you have important guests, make sure that meals are served with ceremony. Food for feasts should be finely decorated. Always surprise your guests with something special. At the end of the meal, offer them a "subtlety"— a little statue made of marzipan.

A grand feast in a knight's castle

What You Do in Your Spare Tim

Knights fight hard, and they like to play hard, too. Hunting wild boar and deer, and catching small birds with trained hawks are favorite pastimes. A knight and his family enjoy listening to music, reading and writing poetry, having picnics, and dancing. Young ladies of the court admire elegant manners and will be charmed by romantic words of love.

Outdoor feast

▲ After hunting, you might be invited to a feast with a lord and his knights. Perhaps noble ladies will join you, too. Servants serve food at an outdoor feast. You should be very helpful to the senior men and to all the ladies. It is a sign of good manners and breeding—very important for a young knight.

Hawking

▼ It's thrilling to watch a hawk swooping to snatch its prey. Trained hawks are very valuable and a sign of high status. Only kings and nobles keep fine sporting birds, such as peregrines and gyrfalcons.

Music and dance

After a feast, there's often dancing in the great hall. You must learn the right dance steps. Paid musicians entertain guests, but a romantic knight learns to play an instrument himself to serenade his sweetheart.

The village fair

► Most villages have at least one local fair every summer, when they celebrate a religious day. Stall-holders sell their produce in the shelter of the castle walls. Officials keep order and look out for thieves and cheats.

A knight and his party out on a hunt

> My hawk is magnificent. Look! She has returned already!

The village fair

Knights and ladies together in the pleasure garden

Ladies in the garden

► Do you like poetry, music, and song? You will enjoy visiting the ladies of the castle in their pleasure garden. It has pretty flowers and fountains, and is also called a "garden of love."

What About the Future?

A knight never loses his fighting spirit. But old age, aches, and pains will eventually stop him from riding off to war. If you survive to old age, you will spend many hours thinking about your death. If you are ill, the doctors and herbalists might be able to make you feel better. Perhaps you will give money to the poor—the church teaches that this is a holy thing to do. You must prepare your will and plan your funeral. You will hire an artist to create a memorial for your tomb.

Medieval remedies

Herbal mixtures

Prayers for healing

Witchcraft and magic

I go to meet my maker.

A good death

▼ The church expects knights to bear pain bravely and to confess their sins. You should forgive your enemies and leave money to help the needy. If you feel ill, doctors will draw some blood from your veins. They think this will make you better—but it won't.

A doctor drawing blood from an ill knight

Sisters of mercy

If you fall ill away from home, ▶ you may be taken to a hospital where monks and nuns care for the ill and for the hungry poor.

Nuns caring for the sick

Tears and mourning

Leeches clean wounds

Purges drive out poisons

Poultices soothe swelling

Friends and family saying farewell to a brave knight

After you die, your body will be placed in a church or in a castle chapel. Mourners will come to comfort your family and friends.

Burial

▶ Priests will say prayers at your funeral, then your body will be buried in the churchyard.

A knight being buried by priests

He fought bravely but he's badly wounded.

A lasting memorial

◀ A craftsman might carve a memorial statue of you. Knights are shown as young and fit, in rich armor. If you are married, include your wife in your memorial.

Your Interview

Answer these questions to test your knowledge, then look at page 32 to find out if you have what it takes to get the job.

Q1 To whom do you owe your loyalty?
A your best friend
B your king
C your wife

Q2 What are tournaments?
A Kitchen gadgets that roast meat
B mock battles, fought for fun
C children's games

Q3 What will you do if you are trapped in a castle siege?
A hide in the cellar
B shelter in the chapel
C fight the enemy for as long as you can

Q4 What are your favorite weapons?
A wooden clubs
B swords and spears
C bows and arrows

Q5 How do you relax in your free time?
A by hunting and hawking
B by painting pictures
C by gardening

Q6 Where do you wear gauntlets?
A under your armor
B on your head
C on your hands

Q7 Which of these is one of your squire's duties?
A helping you put your armor on
B singing in a church choir
C spying on your enemies

Q8 What would you like on your tomb?
A a plain stone slab
B a life-size statue of yourself
C a bunch of flowers

Glossary

Chivalry. A code of good behavior followed by knights. It includes bravery, honesty, loyalty, and showing respect for women.

Coat-of-arms. A design worn on a shield or surcoat. Originally used to identify knights in battle. Later, it became a sign of high rank.

Crusades. Wars fought between medieval knights and Muslim armies, from A.D. 1095 to around 1200. Each side wanted the right to rule the Holy Land—the area around the city of Jerusalem. Crusades were also fought in Spain.

Estate. The castle, land, and farms belonging to a knight.

Gauntlets. Jointed metal gloves worn as part of a suit of armor.

Loot. To steal goods or property during times of war or civil unrest.

Mace. A club with a spiked metal head.

Mail. Armor made of interlinked rings of metal.

Marzipan. A confection of almond paste, sugar, and egg whites that is often shaped into various forms.

Mason. A person skilled in building with stone.

Poultice. A warm mixture (often oatmeal and water) used by medieval doctors to soothe swollen limbs.

Purges. Substances that cleanse a person physically or spiritually.

Quintain. A swinging weight on a tall pole used for practicing fighting skills on horseback.

Siege. Surrounding an enemy castle or town and staying there until the inhabitants must surrender or run out of food.

Squire. A teenage boy who is training to become a knight by being a knight's assistant. From the 14th century on many squires remained in that role because becoming a knight was too expensive.

Surcoat. A cloth covering worn over armor and sometimes decorated with a knight's coat-of-arms.

Tournament. A pretend battle fought for fun. Knights used tournaments for training and to win riches and honor.

Warhorse. A very expensive, specially bred horse, ridden by knights in battle.

Index

A
armor, 3, 11–13, 20, 29, 31

B
battle. *See* warfare

C
castles, 5–6, 18–19, 22–23, 26–27, 29, 31
ceremonies, 11
chivalry, 6, 31. See *also* honor, code of
church, 5, 11, 15, 22, 28–29
coat-of-arms, 6, 20–21, 31
crossbow, 16–17
Crusades, 9, 31

D
death, 6, 9, 16, 18, 28–29

E
entertainment, 20–21, 25–27
estate, 24–25, 31
Europe, 3, 5

F
family, 3, 8–10, 26, 29
feasts, 12, 24–26
foot soldiers, 14, 16–17

G
groom, 6–7, 10, 12

H
helmets, 16
honor, code of, 3, 7, 22, 25
horses, 6, 10, 12, 14, 16, 20–21
warhorses, 3, 12, 31

J
Joan of Arc, 9

K
King Arthur, 6

L
looting, 15, 31
loyalty, 3, 7, 9

M
medicine, 28–29, 31

mercenaries, 7

N
nuns, 5, 28–29

P
peasants, 5, 8, 15, 24–25
plague, 18
priests, 5, 29

S
servants, 8, 24, 26
squire, 6–7, 10–12, 31

T
tournaments, 5, 20–21, 31
training, 9–11, 16, 20

W
warfare, 3, 5–7, 9, 14–17, 22
at sea, 14
siege, 18–19, 31
weapons, 3, 12–13, 16–19, 21
women, 8–9, 21, 26–29

Further Reading

Gravett, Christopher and Dann, Geoff. *Knight (Eyewitness Books)*. Dorling Kindersley Publishing, 2000
Steele, Philipp. *Knight*. Kingfisher, 1998

Did You Get the Job?

Count up your correct answers (below right) and find out.

Your score:

8 Congratulations! Your country needs knights like you.
7 With further training you could become a knight.
5–6 Promising but not good enough yet. Visit a few more tournaments.

3–4 You must be a very young squire.
Fewer than 3 Have you thought about becoming a Roman soldier instead?

1 (B) page 7
2 (B) page 20
3 (C) pages 18–19
4 (B) page 13
5 (A) page 26
6 (C) page 137
7 (A) page 10–11
8 (B) page 29